RECIPES

Every

COLLEGE STUDENT

Should Know

To my children: Joshua, Zachariah, Luke, and Nathaniel, who teach me every day all of the essential lessons that college didn't.

Copyright © 2017 by Quirk Productions, Inc.

Library of Congress Cataloging in Publication Number: 2016941167

ISBN: 978-1-59474-954-4

Printed in China
Typeset in Goudy

Production management by John J. McGurk
Illustration on pages 18–20 by Kate Francis

Quirk Books
215 Church Street
Philadelphia, PA 19106
quirkbooks.com

10 9 8 7 6 5 4 3 2 1

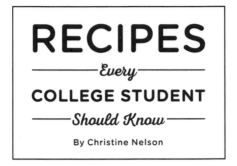

RECIPES

Every

COLLEGE STUDENT

Should Know

By Christine Nelson

QUIRK BOOKS

PHILADELPHIA

Introduction

After years of dreaming about going away to college, you're finally ready. But the questions seem endless. What classes should I take? Should I join a fraternity/sorority? How will I get all this homework done? Should I learn how to cook?

Yes, you should! Learning to cook offers:

1. **Choice.** After years of other people making all the decisions, now it's your turn. You decide what to eat.

2. **Control.** You've probably heard horror stories about the Freshman 15—the pounds a first-year gains. Cooking your own meals gives you control over portions and ingredients.

3. **Knowledge.** That's why you're in college! Even if you forget calculus or Spanish the day after graduation, you will always need to eat. Preparing appetizing, healthy, low-cost meals is a skill you will use for years to come.

4. **Satisfaction.** It's one in the morning, all the stores are closed, and you want a snack. Good thing you can make chocolate-covered popcorn on page 138!

This little book will help get you started with step-by-step recipes, recommended tools, and some kitchen-safety basics. There are meal ideas for a group of friends and quick breakfasts to make before class. This information may not help you pass your history midterm, but it will allow you to eat well while studying for it.

COOKING 101

The Basics

Cooking doesn't need to be complicated. The simple recipes in this book will give you the nourishing food you need to make it through the school year. Pages 24–25 explain the terms you'll need to know. And following these 10 tips will allow you to at least *look* like you know what you're doing.

1. **Buy fresh ingredients.** Read the sell-by dates on dairy, meats, and packaged foods. Look for fruits and vegetables that are not wilted or punctured.

2. **Beware of convenience foods.** Anything already washed, cut up, bagged, or canned may save time, but they're more expensive than whole foods.

3. **Read the recipe through.** Many a home cook has been thwarted by an unexpected instruction to "marinate overnight."

4. **Don't thaw food on the counter.** Ever. (See Safety First! on page 14.)

5. **Follow directions.** Don't just throw all the ingredients together. It won't end well.

6. **Start clean.** Wash your cooking area as well as your hands.

7. **Assemble everything before you start.** You don't want to be in the middle of a recipe when you realize that your roommate drank all the milk.

8. **Measure first.** Peel, chop, measure—whatever it takes to match the ingredients list. Cooking will go more smoothly.

9. **Preheat.** Set the oven to the correct temperature before you start cooking. It will be ready when you are.

10. **Clean as you go.** Post-meal dishes are far more overwhelming than mid-cooking dishes.

Safety First!

Food preparation attracts bacteria, pests, spills, sharp things, hot things, and requests for strange flavor combinations from friends. These basic rules will keep you and the food you prepare safe.

1. **Keep counters, stove, and refrigerator clean.** Wipe up spills promptly. This will help keep the kitchen sanitary and reduce the risk of slipping.

2. **Wash your hands.** Often—before handling food and after every time you handle meat or poultry.

3. **Practice safe handling.** Keep raw meats and poultry separate from other ingredients; refrigerate until ready to use (see box, opposite).

4. **Dress appropriately.** Don't wear loose clothing that could catch fire. Keep long hair tied back. Wear closed-toe shoes to protect your feet from falling pots, knives, and spills.

5. **Keep dish towels and potholders away from hot burners.** Reduce the risk of fire.

6. **Keep a fire extinguisher nearby.** And learn how to use it.

7. **Never leave food unattended.** Be aware of kitchen fires, circling insects, marauding roommates, and other hazards.

8. **Always use pot holders.** Notably when handling hot dishes or anything that steams.

9. **Be aware of what's on the burner.** Keep pot handles turned inward on the stove. While stirring liquids, stir away from your body.

10. **Sharpen knives.** Learn how to use knives properly. A dull knife is more dangerous than a sharp one because it's more likely to slip.

Safe Food Handling

Always thaw food in the refrigerator. To speed it up, you can put frozen food in a sealed plastic bag and set it in a bowl of cold water. Change water every 30 minutes until food is thawed. You can also use a microwave's defrost setting. Food thawed by either method must be cooked immediately.

Minimum Cooking Temperatures

These are the recommendations on Food-Safety.gov. Use your thermometer!

Food	Temperature (°F)
Beef, pork, veal, lamb	160
Turkey, chicken	165
Steaks, roasts, chops	145
Poultry breasts, roasts	165
Fresh pork	145
Fresh ham (to cook)	145
Cooked ham (to reheat)	140
Leftovers	165
Casseroles	165
Finfish	145, or until flesh is opaque and flakes easily with a fork

What to Stock

Here's what to have on hand for the recipes in this book.

In the Pantry:

- Ground coffee
- Tea bags
- Sugar
- Salt
- Ground cinnamon
- Ground paprika
- Black pepper
- Italian seasoning
- Cooking spray
- Bread
- Old-fashioned oats
- Peanut butter
- Raisins
- Granola
- Honey
- Canned tuna, chicken, and/or ham
- Taco seasoning
- All-purpose flour
- Baking powder
- Baking soda
- Popcorn kernels
- Olive oil
- Canola oil
- Balsamic vinegar

In the Refrigerator:

- Butter
- Eggs
- Milk
- Half-and-half
- Ketchup
- Bacon
- Jam
- Yogurt
- Relish
- Mayonnaise
- Mustard
- Minced garlic

Tools, Etc.

In addition to a stove and microwave, here is the basic equipment you will need to set up a small kitchen and make most recipes, including the ones in this book.

Slicing and Dicing*

a. 8- to 10-inch chef's knife (for meat, vegetables, mincing)
b. 8- to 10-inch serrated knife (for breads, pizza, pies, tomatoes)
c. 3½- to 5-inch paring knife (for peeling and cutting small fruits and vegetables)
d. knife sharpener
e. vegetable peeler
f. 2 plastic cutting boards (one for meat only)
g. 1 wooden cutting board

---

* **Note:** Never place good knives in the dishwasher. Sharpen them frequently for optimal slicing and dicing.

Prepping

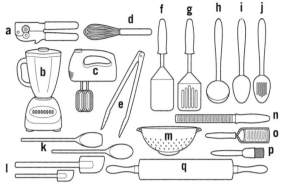

a. can opener
b. blender
c. electric hand mixer (optional)
d. whisk
e. pair tongs
f. flexible spatula
g. nonflexible spatula
h. ladle
i. large spoon
j. slotted spoon
k. 2 wooden spoons

l. 2 rubber spatulas, small and large
m. colander
n. microplane grater for zesting
o. cheese grater
p. heatproof brush
q. rolling pin

Measuring

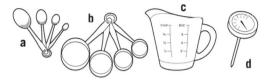

a. 1 set measuring spoons
b. 1 set dry-ingredient measuring cups
c. 1 liquid measuring cup
d. 1 instant-read meat thermometer

Cooking and Baking

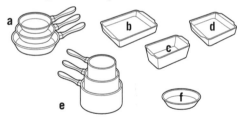

a. 3 nonstick skillets/frying pans: 8-, 10-, and 12-inch
b. 1 9-by-13-inch baking pan
c. 1 8-by-4-inch loaf pan
d. 1 8- or 9-inch square baking pan
e. 3 saucepans: 1½ quart, 3 or 4 quart, and 4½ to 5 quart
f. 1 9-inch pie plate

Other Dorm-Kitchen Essentials

- Set of serving ware: dishes, cups, glasses, utensils
- Pot holders (2)
- Dish towels (2)
- Sponges (2)
- Dish soap
- Drying rack
- Coffeepot
- Corkscrew
- Zip-top plastic bags, assorted sizes
- Airtight plastic containers with lids
- Paper towels
- Plastic wrap
- Aluminum foil
- Wax or parchment paper

Healthy Eating

Just by cooking your own meals, you are eating health-ier, avoiding packaged foods and calorie-heavy restau-rant meals. With a little research and some practice, you can create a nutritious baseline meal plan that works for you. To start, follow these recommendations from ChooseMyPlate.gov to eat healthier:

1. **"Focus on variety, amount, and nutrition."** According to Health.gov, men aged 18 to 25 should consume 2,400 to 3,200 calories per day and women aged 18 to 25 should consume 1,800 to 2,400, depending on how active you are. Aim for somewhere in those ranges, and choose a variety of nutritious fruits, vegetables, grains, proteins, and dairy.

2. **"Choose foods and beverages with less saturated fat, sodium, and added sugars."** Read—and understand—those labels!

3. **"Start with small changes to build healthier eating styles."** Maybe the thought of a full diet overhaul overwhelms you, but you could start with one new healthy habit. Add a smoothie at breakfast or a green vegetable at lunch for starters.

4. **"Support healthy eating for everyone."** When your dormmates want to stop drinking soda, back them up. When you see a petition for the dining hall to serve more vegetables, sign it. Does your campus have an organization dedicated to combating food insecurity in your city? Join in. The more access a community has to healthy choices, the better it is for everyone.

Meal Planning

Don't find yourself studying on an empty stomach! Schedule a regular planning day to figure out meals for the week ahead. Choose the recipes you want to make. Check what's already in your fridge. Make a grocery list. Shop. Cook! You'll never go hungry again.

Terms to Know

Here are some of the most basic cooking terms you're likely to come across as you explore the gigantic world of recipes . . . and this book.

Boil: Heat liquid until large bubbles form on the surface, often done on the stove in a pan with a lid on it.

Broil: Cook food quickly by placing it directly under or above high heat.

Chop: Use a knife to cut food into medium-sized pieces. If a recipe says to *dice*, cut the pieces so they are perfectly matching in size.

Coat: Completely cover a food in an ingredient, such as flour.

Combine: Stir ingredients together until they are evenly distributed.

Dice: Cut food into small uniform pieces, about $1/8$ to $1/4$ inch around.

Flake: Break off small pieces of food with a fork. If a food is cooked properly, it should flake easily.

Fry: Cook food in oil, butter, or other fat in a hot pan over direct heat until browned.

Microwave: Cook in a microwave for a specific time at a specific heat level.

Mince: Use a knife to cut food in the smallest pieces possible, smaller than if you were to chop it.

Panfry: Cooking food quickly in a hot pan with a fat, such as oil or butter; similar to sautéing, but generally uses more fat and creates more browning (used for steak, pork chops, fish).

Reserve: Set aside an amount to be used later. For example, "reserve $1/2$ cup of the cooking water" means pouring $1/2$ cup of the water from the pot into a cup or bowl before draining the rest of the pot.

Sauté: Cook food quickly in a hot pan with a small amount of fat, such as oil or butter.

Sear: Quickly brown or char food over very high heat.

Simmer: Cook food in water over low heat. There may be small bubbles, but not a full boil.

Slice: Cut food into strips.

QUICK
BREAKFASTS

A Quick Cup of Tea

	1
	serving

If you can boil water, you can brew a quick cup of tea. Coffee's less jumpy cousin is perfect for when you want to put your feet up and enjoy something hot to drink.

    8 to 10 ounces water, or enough to fill your mug
    1 tea bag
    1 tablespoon milk, or to taste, optional
    1 to 2 teaspoons sugar or honey, or to taste,
        optional

1. Pour water into a small saucepan and cover.

2. Place saucepan over high heat. Heat for about 5 to 6 minutes, until water comes to a boil. Large bubbles will form and break on top of the water.

3. Place tea bag in mug, pour water over tea bag, and let steep. (How long? See "Approximate Steep Times," opposite.)

4. Remove tea bag immediately after steeping, or it will make the tea bitter. Add milk and sugar or honey (if desired).

Elective Equipment: If you want to try brewing tea with loose tea leaves, purchase disposable tea bags or a tea ball (a metal ball covered with tiny holes that holds tea leaves). Use it to follow the above instructions. Always empty and rinse the tea ball immediately after use so the tea leaves don't dry onto the sides and become a science experiment. At least once a week, clean by hand with dish soap or place in the cutlery section of a dishwasher and wash.

Approximate Steep Times	
Black tea	5 minutes
Green tea	3 minutes
Fruit/herbal tea	7 minutes

A Great Cup of Coffee

 Yield varies

Start with a medium roast of your favorite brand. After making a few pots, you should feel confident enough to experiment with the brand, roast, amount of coffee and/or water, and brew time.

Automatic-Drip Coffee

1. Fill the water reservoir.

2. Place a filter—either a reusable mesh filter or an unbleached paper filter—in the basket.

3. Add 1 tablespoon ground coffee per 1 cup water.

4. Start the machine and brew according to the manufacturer's instructions.

French Press Coffee

1. Boil enough water to fill the carafe.

2. Put desired amount of grounds in the carafe. Start with 1 tablespoon per 1 cup water.

3. Pour boiling water into the carafe.

4. Put the lid on the carafe, but leave the plunger up. Let stand for 5 minutes.

5. Gently press the plunger down. Pour the coffee.

Iced Coffee

1. After brewing coffee via either of the above methods, remove it from the heat source, otherwise the coffee will burn.

2. Let coffee cool to room temperature. If you make it the night before, it will be room temperature when you get up.

3. Prepare coffee with milk and sugar, as you like.

4. Fill a glass with 6 to 12 ice cubes and pour coffee over them.

Eggs

1
serving

Eggs are a great, inexpensive source of protein. Their natural habitat is the breakfast table, but they can be eaten at any meal—even as snacks.

Hard-Boiled Eggs

> 2 eggs
> Salt to taste
> Ground black pepper to taste

1. Place eggs in a small saucepan along with water to cover them by no more than an inch.

2. Bring to a boil over high heat.

3. Turn off heat and cover pot tightly with a lid. Let stand on burner for 10 minutes.

4. Drain water and gently shake pan to crack the eggshells. Fill pan halfway with cold water and about 12 ice cubes.

5. Let eggs stand in the cold water for about 5 minutes. Peel shells.

6. Enjoy with salt and pepper to taste.

Fried Eggs (Sunny Side Up)

Cooking spray or 1 tablespoon butter
2 eggs
Pinch of salt
Pinch of ground black pepper

1. Coat a medium-sized frying pan with cooking spray or butter. Heat pan over medium-low heat for 3 minutes.

2. While pan heats, gently crack eggs into a cup, being careful not to break the yolks. Using a cup instead of cracking them directly onto the pan is the easiest way to evenly cook both at the same time.

3. Pour eggs into hot pan. Cover and cook for about 3 minutes, or until whites are opaque and no longer runny.

4. Tilt the pan over a plate and slide eggs onto its surface. Season with salt and pepper; serve.

Scrambled Eggs

2 eggs
1 tablespoon half-and-half
Pinch of salt
Pinch of ground black pepper
Cooking spray

1. In a small bowl beat eggs, half-and-half, salt, and pepper with a fork until thoroughly mixed.

2. Spray a small frying pan with cooking spray. Heat it over medium-low heat for about 2 minutes.

3. Pour egg mixture into prepared pan. Using a heat-resistant spatula, stir eggs, scraping along bottom and sides of pan, until eggs begin to clump, about 2 minutes.

4. When no liquid remains, remove pan from heat. Use the spatula to transfer eggs to a plate and serve.

Egg Sandwich

□■　1
sandwich

When your stomach is rumbling loud enough for the professor to hear, you'll realize that Mom was right: Breakfast really *is* the most important meal of the day. With this recipe you can make your stomach happy in less than five minutes.

Cooking spray
1 egg
Pinch of salt
Pinch of ground black pepper
2 slices bread, 1 English muffin, or 1 bagel
1 slice cheese
1 slice ham
Ketchup (optional)

1. Spray a microwavable cup with cooking spray. Crack egg into cup. Sprinkle with salt and pepper. With a fork, beat egg until thoroughly mixed. Microwave on high power for 1 minute. The egg should look dry without runny bits. If it doesn't, microwave for 10 seconds at a time until done.

2. While egg is cooking, toast bread on the light to medium setting.

3. Layer egg, cheese, and ham on a slice of toast. Spread ketchup, if desired, on the other slice and close sandwich. Eat immediately.

Elective Equipment: Microwavable egg bowls with an attached lid are available in home-goods stores. These keep the egg from exploding in the microwave. You can accomplish the same thing by putting a microwaveable dish on top of the cup.

Tip: Add a piece of fruit for a more complete meal.

Breakfast Burritos

2
burritos

Make this breakfast wrap on mornings when you're in a hurry and don't have time to sit and eat. Even better: make it the night before and pop it in the microwave for about 30 seconds before heading out to class.

Cooking spray (if you're using a stove)
1 cup frozen diced potatoes with onion and
    peppers
2 teaspoons canola oil (if you're using a microwave)
4 eggs
Pinch of salt
Pinch of ground black pepper
$1/3$ cup shredded cheese
$1/4$ cup salsa
2 tortillas

On the stove:

1. Coat a medium-sized skillet with cooking spray and heat over medium-high heat for about $1^1/_2$ minutes.

2. Carefully add frozen vegetables in an even layer. Cover and cook, turning with a spatula every 2 to 3 minutes, for a total of 7 to 10 minutes, until light golden brown. Transfer to a bowl.

3. Wipe the pan with paper towels and coat again with cooking spray.

4. In a bowl, whisk eggs with salt and pepper. Add to skillet and scramble as on page 34.

In the microwave:

1. Place frozen vegetables in a microwave-safe bowl. Add canola oil, salt, and pepper. Toss with a spoon until vegetables are evenly coated.

2. Cover bowl with plastic wrap and punch a hole in the middle of the plastic with a knife or your finger.

3. Microwave on high power for 10 minutes. Set aside.

4. Place eggs in a microwave-safe bowl. Scramble eggs according to the microwave instructions on page 35.

To assemble:

1. In the center of each tortilla, layer half of the eggs, vegetables, cheese, and salsa in a vertical line.

2. To roll burritos, fold the bottom quarter of the tortilla toward the top and over the filling.

3. Fold in the left third of the tortilla toward the center, then fold the right third in over it.

4. Fold down the top to close burrito. Pick it up, holding the bottom and the front seam closed.

Breakfast Bowls: If you're not in the mood for tortillas, you can enjoy the filling alone. Just divide the cooked ingredients equally between two bowls and mix thoroughly.

Bacon

3
slices

Believe it or not, bacon can be cooked in the microwave, saving you from dirtying (and washing) a pan. The taste is the same whether you microwave or panfry bacon, though panfried has an added benefit: bacon grease, which makes a fried egg (see page 33) even tastier. After you're finished cooking the bacon, use the same pan to cook your eggs and skip the cooking spray.

   3 thick slices bacon

In the microwave:

1. Line a microwave-safe plate with 3 sheets of paper towel. Arrange bacon on top and cover with 2 more sheets of paper towel.

2. Microwave on high power for $3^1/_2$ minutes. Bacon should be steaming and browned on the edges. If not, continue to cook for 10-second intervals until it is.

On the stove:

1. Heat a medium-sized frying pan over medium heat for 1 minute.

2. Lower heat to medium-low, place bacon in pan, and cover. After 1 minute, use a spatula to lift slices to make sure they are not sticking to pan. Cook for about $1\frac{1}{2}$ minutes more. Flip and cook for a final $1\frac{1}{2}$ minutes.

"Life expectancy would grow by leaps and bounds if green vegetables smelled as good as bacon."

—*Doug Larson*

Oatmeal in a Mug

Surely you've heard that oatmeal is a great source of protein and fiber. It also makes a filling breakfast that will satisfy you until lunchtime. Cook it in the microwave or on a stove—there's no difference in taste or texture. Customize with mix-ins to your taste.

> 1/2 cup old-fashioned rolled oats
> 1 cup milk or water
> 2 teaspoons sugar, or to taste
> Pinch of salt

1. In a microwave-safe mug (bowl), stir ingredients together to combine. Microwave on high power for 2 1/2 minutes.

2. Continue to cook in 20-second intervals, stirring after each, until oatmeal rises to top. Oatmeal is done when almost all liquid is absorbed and the mixture looks creamy. Cool slightly before eating.

Stovetop Option:

In a small saucepan, stir ingredients together. Cook over medium heat until mixture starts to boil (about 3 minutes). Lower heat to medium-low and cook for about 4 to 5 minutes, or until most liquid is absorbed and mixture looks creamy. Remove from heat and let cool before eating.

Mix-Ins

- Apples, bananas, nuts

- Cinnamon and raisins

- Peanut Butter (add in step 1)

- Diced fruits

- Seeds (sunflower, chia)

Yogurt Parfait

1
parfait

For a fraction of the cost of a store-bought parfait, you can make your own—just the way you want it, with your favorite combination of ingredients. Budget hint: a 32-ounce container of plain yogurt is usually cheaper than the small, single-serving size.

1 cup yogurt, flavor of your choice
1 cup fresh fruit
1/3 cup granola

1. In a tall glass layer one-third of the yogurt, one-third of the fruit, and one-third of the granola. Repeat to make 2 more layers, ending with the granola.

Parfait to Impress: Layer your parfait in a wine glass for a fancy addition to brunch.

Fruit Poppers

| 1
serving

A cool yummy treat for breakfast-time, summer-time, anytime.

> Assorted fruit (bananas, strawberries, grapes),
>   sliced or kept whole
> 1 container plain or flavored yogurt

1. Dip fruit slices into yogurt to coat. (It may be helpful to use a toothpick.) Place slices on wax paper laid on a plate or baking sheet. Freeze for at least 1 hour. Pop in your mouth!

Extra-special option: Keep the fruit whole and roll in granola or chopped nuts after coating with yogurt. (This works especially well with bananas.) Freeze as directed, slice, and enjoy!

Smoothie My Way

	1
	smoothie

Don't wake your roommate with the blender!

Yogurt Smoothie

1 cup plain or flavored yogurt
1 cup milk
1 cup ice
Mix-ins of your choice (see list, opposite)

1. Combine all ingredients in a blender and process until smooth. Pour into a cup and enjoy.

Non-Dairy Smoothie

2 cups orange juice
$1/4$ cup honey
2 ripe bananas
Mix-ins of your choice, optional (see opposite)

1. Combine all ingredients in a blender and process until smooth. Pour into a cup and enjoy.

Mix-Ins

Make this quick and healthful meal even more filling with any of these tasty additions.

- 2 tablespoons peanut butter and 1 medium banana
- 2 tablespoons hazelnut spread and 1 medium banana
- 1 cup strawberries, hulled and halved (to hull, cut around the stem and leaves with the tip of a sharp knife, then pull out stem)
- 1 cup blueberries, stems removed
- 1 cup drained canned peaches
- 1 cup drained canned pears and $\frac{1}{4}$ cup almonds
- 1 cup drained pineapple chunks and $\frac{1}{4}$ cup shredded coconut
- $\frac{1}{2}$ cup dried cranberries and $\frac{1}{4}$ cup chopped walnuts
- 1 medium ripe mango, peeled and chopped

TO-GO
LUNCHES

Egg Salad Sandwich

1
sandwich

Often you won't have enough time between classes to go back to your room or to the dining hall for a bite to eat. This problem is easily solved by packing it to go.

2 hard-boiled eggs (see page 32), sliced
1 tablespoon minced onion (see Tip)
1 tablespoon relish
Pinch of salt
Pinch of ground black pepper
1 tablespoon mayonnaise
1 leaf romaine lettuce
2 slices whole wheat bread
2 slices cheese

1. In a small bowl, mash eggs. Add onion, relish, salt, pepper, and mayonnaise. Mix until well combined.

2. Place lettuce on one slice of bread, stack a slice of cheese on top, and spread egg mixture on cheese. Top with remaining cheese and bread.

3. Optional step for eating on the go: Wrap sandwich tightly in plastic wrap. As you eat, unwrap a small section at time. This helps keep all of the filling between the bread, where it belongs, rather than on your keyboard.

Tip: *Mince* means to use a knife to cut an ingredient as small as you can.

Hummus and Veggie Wraps

2
wraps

These two ingredients make a great healthy snack. Wrap them up for an easy-to-transport option for when you're on the go.

1 green bell pepper
$^1/_2$ onion
1 cup mushrooms
2 tortillas
$^1/_2$ cup hummus

1. With a sharp knife, slice the top and bottom off the pepper. Carefully cut out seeds and discard them. Slice pepper into strips.

2. Slice onion into strips (see box, opposite).

3. Slice each mushroom, depending on thickness, into 4 to 6 slices.

4. Spread half the hummus on each tortilla. Arrange half of the peppers, onions, and mushrooms on

each. Fold tortillas closed and wrap in plastic wrap until ready to eat.

How to Slice an Onion

With a large knife, cut off the top and root ends. Remove the outer papery layer. Keeping your fingers out of the way, slice as thick as you'd like. Store leftover onion in a plastic bag in the refrigerator for 2 to 3 days.

Tuna Sub

1
sandwich

Is this incredible sandwich a sub, hoagie, hero, or grinder? The answer depends on your location; most of its names are regional. Whatever you call it, a sandwich of tasty fillings in a long roll makes an excellent meal.

1 5-ounce can tuna in water, drained (see Tip)
1 tablespoon minced onion
$1/4$ cup minced celery
Pinch of salt
Pinch of ground black pepper
1 tablespoon mayonnaise
1 long sandwich roll
1 leaf romaine lettuce
2 slices cheese

1. Place tuna in a small bowl. With a fork, flake it into small pieces. Add onion, celery, salt, pepper, and mayonnaise. Mix until combined.

2. With a serrated or bread knife, slice the roll lengthwise about three-quarters of the way through, leaving the opposite side uncut. Open the roll like a
   book and place lettuce, cheese, and tuna mixture
   inside. Close roll and wrap in plastic wrap until
   ready to eat.

Tip: To drain water from tuna, open the can and,
while holding it over the sink, gently press the lid
into the fish and pour off the liquid.

Taco Wrap

2
wraps

Everyone loves tacos. Meat, cheese, and salsa—
what could be better?

Cooking spray
$1/2$ pound lean ground beef or other ground meat
2 tablespoons ($1/2$ packet) taco seasoning
2 tortillas
$2/3$ cup shredded cheddar cheese
3 tablespoons salsa
3 tablespoons sour cream
1 cup shredded lettuce

1. Coat a medium-sized skillet with cooking spray and
   heat over medium heat for 1 minute.

2. Lower heat to medium-low, and add meat. Cook,
   using a spatula to break apart, for about 6 minutes,
   or until meat is no longer pink.

3. Remove from heat. Add seasoning and $1/3$ cup water. Stir until combined and thickened.

4. On each tortilla, spread half of the filling, cheese, salsa, sour cream, and lettuce. Close wraps. Serve immediately.

Make-Ahead Option: Let wrap cool to room temperature and cover in plastic wrap. When you're ready to heat, remove plastic and microwave each for about 1 minute on high power. The taco also tastes fine at room temperature if no microwave is handy.

Bacon and Guacamole Wrap

1
wrap

Avocado: incredibly healthy. Bacon: not so healthy. Avocado and bacon together: incredibly delicious.

   $^1/_2$ cup guacamole
   1 tortilla
   3 slices pepper jack cheese
   3 slices cooked bacon (see page 40), cooled

1. Spread guacamole on tortilla. Layer cheese on top of guacamole.

2. Place bacon on top of cheese. Fold the top and bottom of the tortilla toward the middle. Then roll tortilla from left to right to close. Wrap in plastic wrap until ready to eat.

Tip: Pack your lunch with a reusable frozen ice-pack to keep your drink cold and your sandwich fresh.

Chicken Salad Sandwich

| 1 |
| *sandwich* |

This is a great use for leftover cooked chicken breast.

1 5-ounce can chunk white chicken in water,
    drained, or $1/2$ cup chopped cooked chicken
$1/4$ cup minced celery
Pinch of salt
Pinch of paprika
1 tablespoon mayonnaise
2 slices raisin bread
2 slices provolone cheese
$1/4$ medium-sized apple, thinly sliced

1. Place chicken in a small bowl. Add celery, salt, paprika, and mayonnaise. Mix until combined.

2. On a slice of bread, layer a slice of cheese, half of the apple slices, chicken mixture, the remaining apple slices, and the other slice of cheese. Close sandwich and wrap in plastic wrap until lunch.

Buffalo Chicken Sandwich

1
sandwich

If you wish the spirit of Saturday football games could be with you all week long, try this sandwich.

    2 tablespoons cream cheese, softened
    1 tablespoon buffalo wing sauce
    1 5-ounce can chunk white chicken in water,
        drained, or $1/2$ cup chopped cooked chicken
    1 round roll
    2 slices mozzarella cheese
    1 leaf romaine lettuce

1. Place softened cream cheese and sauce in a medium-sized bowl. Mix until well combined.

2. Add chicken and use a fork to break it into small pieces. Mix until all ingredients are well combined.

3. Slice roll in half. On the bottom stack lettuce, 1 slice of cheese, chicken mixture, and the other slice of cheese. Close sandwich and wrap in plastic wrap until ready to eat.

Italian Hoagie

| 1 |
| *sandwich* |

This Philadelphia lunch staple will keep you going through a busy afternoon.

1 long sandwich roll
1 tablespoon mayonnaise
3 slices provolone cheese
3 slices salami
3 slices peppered ham
3 slices sandwich-size pepperoni
$1/2$ cup shredded lettuce
$1/4$ cup very thinly sliced onions
1 tablespoon olive oil
Pinch of oregano

1. With a serrated knife, slice the roll lengthwise about three-quarters of the way through. Open the roll and spread a thin layer of mayonnaise inside.

2. Place cheese and meats on bread. Spread lettuce and onion on top. Sprinkle on oil and oregano. Close the roll. Keep in plastic wrap until ready to eat.

Chicken Apple Salad

1
serving

Raisins, apples, honey—this salad is practically a dessert. In fact, offer your friends a dessert salad and see what they say, just for science.

 $1/4$ head lettuce
 1 cup chopped cooked chicken
 $1/4$ cup raisins
 $1/2$ cup apple slices
 Honey Mustard Dressing (page 67) to taste

1. Wash and dry lettuce (see page 66). With clean hands or a knife, tear or cut lettuce into bite-sized pieces. Place in a salad bowl.

2. Top with chicken, raisins, and apples.

3. Toss with dressing and serve.

Greek Salad

| 1 |
serving

This rich, savory salad is a far cry from the taste-less offerings at a dining hall salad bar. Add cooked chicken to make it even heartier.

$1/4$ head lettuce
$1/2$ cup feta cheese
$1/4$ cup kalamata olives
$1/2$ cup cucumber slices
$1/2$ cup grape tomatoes halved lengthwise
$1/4$ cup sliced red onions
Balsamic Vinaigrette (page 67) to taste

1. Wash and dry lettuce (see page 66). With clean hands or a knife, tear or cut lettuce into bite-sized pieces. Place in a salad bowl.

2. Top with feta, olives, cucumbers, tomatoes, and onions.

3. Toss with vinaigrette and serve.

Two Healthy Salads

1

serving each

Salads are a foolproof way to include more vegetables, fruits, and leafy greens in your diet. Try these twists on the usual bowl of boring lettuce.

Mozzarella and Cranberry

$^{1}/_{4}$ head lettuce
$^{1}/_{2}$ cup shredded mozzarella cheese
$^{1}/_{4}$ cup dried cranberries
$^{1}/_{4}$ cup chopped walnuts
Raspberry Vinaigrette dressing (page 68) to taste

1. Wash and dry lettuce (see page 66). With clean hands or a knife, tear or cut into bite-sized pieces. Place in a bowl.

2. Top with mozzarella, cranberries, and walnuts.

3. Toss with vinaigrette and serve.

Avocado and Sunflower Seeds

$1/4$ head lettuce
1 avocado, chopped
$1/2$ cucumber, chopped
Sunflower seeds to taste
Balsamic Vinaigrette (page 67) to taste

1. Wash and dry lettuce (see page 66). With clean hands or a knife, tear or cut into bite-sized pieces. Place in a bowl.

2. Top with avocado, cucumbers, and sunflower seeds.

3. Toss with vinaigrette and serve.

How to Wash Lettuce

Given how healthy leafy greens are, you might be shocked to learn that they can be harmful, too. Because plants like lettuce, kale, collards, and spinach grow close to the ground, they're susceptible to bacteria from irrigation systems. Always wash greens, even if you buy them bagged.

1. Remove leaves individually and rinse them under water, gently rubbing them with your fingers to remove dirt. Alternatively, you can swirl them in a large bowl of water, letting dirt sink to the bottom, or use a salad spinner (see package directions for proper use). Drain and repeat.

2. Shake remaining water off leaves.

3. Place leaves on a clean kitchen towel or paper towels and allow to dry thoroughly. Blot them if necessary.

4. Store leftover washed and dried leaves. Roll them gently in paper towels and place in a zip-top plastic bag; refrigerate until ready to use.

DIY Dressings

Honey Mustard Dressing

In addition to being a perfect salad topper—tangy! sweet! addictive!—this dressing makes a wonderful dip or sauce for everything from chicken to vegetables. *Makes $1/4$ cup.*

  1 tablespoon honey
  1 tablespoon Dijon mustard
  1 tablespoon lime juice
  $1/4$ cup canola oil
  $1/4$ teaspoon salt or to taste

1. In a small bowl combine ingredients and whisk until smooth. Serve. Refrigerate any leftovers, covered, for up to 3 days.

Balsamic Vinaigrette

The quality of your ingredients will shine through in this recipe. So if you have a bottle of fancy balsamic vinegar or quality olive oil, use it! Experiment with adding fresh or dried herbs, such as basil or parsley, to this dressing. Just let it rest for an hour or so before serving, so that the flavors have time to combine. *Makes ¹/₄ cup.*

   ¹/₄ cup olive oil
   1 tablespoon balsamic vinegar
   ¹/₈ teaspoon salt or to taste
   ¹/₈ teaspoon pepper or to taste

1. In a small bowl, combine ingredients and whisk until smooth. Refrigerate leftovers, covered, for up to 3 days.

Raspberry Vinaigrette

If you like a sweeter edge to your salad, this dressing is for you. *Makes about ³/₄ cup.*

   ¹/₄ cup fresh or defrosted frozen raspberries
   1 tablespoon sugar
   2 tablespoons balsamic vinegar
   ¹/₂ cup olive oil
   1 tablespoon honey
   ¹/₂ teaspoon salt
   ¹/₄ teaspoon black pepper

1. In a small bowl mix raspberries and sugar. Let stand for about 15 minutes. Mash with a fork.

2. Add remaining ingredients. Whisk with a wire whisk until blended, or put mixture in a blender and puree until smooth. Serve. Refrigerate any leftovers, covered, for up to 3 days.

"The perfect dressing is essential to the perfect salad, and I see no reason whatsoever for using a bottled dressing, which may have been sitting on the grocery shelf for weeks, even months—even years."

—Julia Child

COOK ONCE,
EAT TWICE

Tacos *and* Sloppy Joes

| ⊞ ⬜ | 2 *tacos* | 2 *sandwiches* |

Cooking the meat for both of these tasty meals at once makes the second dinner a cinch.

Tacos

Cooking spray
1 pound ground beef
$1/2$ onion, minced
1 1.25-ounce packet taco seasoning
1 cup shredded lettuce
$1/4$ cup salsa
$1/2$ cup shredded cheddar cheese
$1/4$ cup sour cream
2 taco shells

1. Coat a medium-sized skillet with cooking spray and heat it over medium heat for 1 minute.

2. Lower heat to medium-low. Add meat and onions. Cook, breaking meat apart with a wooden spatula, for about 6 minutes, until meat is no longer pink.

3. Remove from heat. Add taco seasoning and $1/3$ cup water. Stir until sauce thickens.

4. Transfer half of the meat mixture to a container and let cool. Cover and refrigerate for up to 4 days.

5. On a microwave-safe plate, microwave taco shells on high power for 45 seconds. Divide remaining meat, lettuce, salsa, cheese, and sour cream between taco shells and enjoy immediately.

Sloppy Joes

Reserved meat mixture from tacos
$1/3$ cup barbecue sauce
$1/2$ cup shredded cheddar cheese
2 hamburger rolls

1. In a medium-sized skillet, heat reserved meat mixture and barbecue sauce over medium heat for about 5 minutes, until heated through.

2. Place half of the meat mixture on the bottom of each roll. Sprinkle each with half of the cheese, close rolls, and serve immediately.

Chicken Chili *and* Chicken Casserole

| 2 servings chili | 2 servings caserole |

Both of these meals are great for a hearty appetite. Because of the low-fat proteins, they are satisfying without being too heavy. Serve them with your favorite salad.

Chicken Chili

2 tablespoons olive oil, divided

1 pound chicken breast

1 teaspoon minced garlic

$1/3$ cup minced onion

1 tablespoon Italian seasoning

1 medium zucchini, peeled and chopped

1 15-ounce can diced tomatoes

$1/2$ 15-ounce can red kidney beans

1 8-ounce can tomato sauce

$1/2$ teaspoon salt, or to taste

1. In a large skillet, heat 1 tablespoon of the oil over medium-high heat for 1 minute. Add chicken and cover. Cook for 8 minutes per side, or until no longer pink in the center. Transfer to a plate, let cool, and chop into bite-sized pieces.

2. Add the rest of the ingredients to skillet and cook on low heat for 30 minutes. Add chicken and cook for an additional 30 minutes.

3. Transfer half of the mixture to a container and let cool. Cover and refrigerate for up to 3 days for use in casserole (below). Serve the remaining chili while still warm.

Chicken Casserole

Cooking spray
8 ounces medium-sized pasta such as bow-tie
Reserved Chicken Chili mixture
8 ounces shredded cheddar cheese

1. Preheat oven to 350°F and spray a 13-by-9-inch baking pan with cooking spray. In a 5-quart saucepan, bring $2^1/_2$ quarts of water to a boil.

2. Add pasta and cook according to the package directions. Drain and return pasta to saucepan.

3. Add chili and cheese to pasta and use a spoon to toss until incorporated. Transfer mixture to the prepared pan and bake for 30 minutes, or until cheese is melted and bubbly. Serve warm.

Sausage with Vegetables *and* Sausage Pie

| |
| 2 servings sausage | 2 servings pie |

For lighter versions that don't skimp on taste, substitute Italian-seasoned turkey sausage for the pork sausage.

Sausage with Vegetables

2 tablespoons olive oil, divided

4 dinner-sized pork sausage links
   (about ¹/₂ pound total)

2 medium green bell peppers

1 yellow onion, sliced

10 ounces sliced mushrooms

1 teaspoon minced garlic

¹/₂ teaspoon salt

1 teaspoon Italian seasoning

2 tablespoons balsamic vinegar

1 tablespoon honey

1. In a medium skillet, heat 1 tablespoon of the oil over medium-high heat for 1 minute. Lower heat to medium and add sausages. Cook, turning about every 2 minutes, until internal temperature is 160°F.

2. Transfer 2 sausages to a container and let cool. Cover and refrigerate for up to 3 days for use in Sausage Pie. Slice remaining sausages into bite-sized rounds.

3. Slice peppers, onions, and mushrooms into strips and put in skillet with remaining oil. Add garlic, salt, Italian seasoning, vinegar, and honey. Cook and stir frequently until vegetables are soft, about 10 minutes.

4. Place 1 cup vegetables in container and cool. Cover and refrigerate for up to 3 days for use in Sausage Pie (opposite).

5. Combine sliced sausage and remaining vegetables. Enjoy warm.

Sausage Pie

Cooking spray
1 pound potatoes, peeled and chopped
$\frac{1}{4}$ cup grated Parmesan cheese
1 teaspoon salt, divided, or to taste
Reserved cooked sausages and vegetables
1 8-ounce can diced tomatoes, drained

1. Preheat oven to 350°F. Spray a loaf pan with cooking spray.

2. Place potatoes in a medium saucepan and cover with water. Bring to a boil over high heat and cook until potatoes are easily broken with fork. Drain, reserving $\frac{1}{3}$ cup of the cooking liquid. Transfer potatoes to a medium-sized bowl and mash with cooking liquid, cheese, and $\frac{1}{2}$ teaspoon salt.

3. Dice sausages. Place them in a saucepan with vegetables, tomatoes, and $\frac{1}{2}$ teaspoon salt. Cook over medium heat until liquid is absorbed.

4. Spread meat mixture on bottom of the prepared pan and cover with mashed potatoes. Bake for 20 minutes and serve.

Pork Stew *and* Pork Wraps

2	2
servings stew	*wraps*

These Tex-Mex-inspired standards are not only full of flavor, they're key for finals week. Make the stew when you're home studying; it only takes a few minutes, and you can hit the books while it simmers. The wraps will come together in the crunch time between exams.

Pork Stew

    1 tablespoon olive oil

    1 pound pork loin, chopped

    1 small onion, minced

    2 teaspoons minced garlic

    1 medium zucchini, peeled and chopped

    1 1.25-ounce packet taco seasoning

    1 cup mild chunky salsa

    1 cup canned pink beans, drained

1. In a large saucepan, heat oil over medium heat for 1 minute. Add pork, onions, and garlic. Cook,

stirring frequently, for about 6 to 8 minutes, until meat is browned.

2. Add remaining ingredients and simmer over low heat for 1 hour.

3. Transfer 1 cup of the stew to a container and let cool. Cover and refrigerate for up to 3 days for use in Pork Wraps (below). Serve remaining stew warm.

Pork Wraps

Reserved Pork Stew
1/4 cup instant brown rice
1/2 teaspoon butter
1/2 cup shredded cheddar cheese
2 tortillas

1. In a medium saucepan combine rice, 1/2 cup water, and butter. Cook according to package directions.

2. Microwave stew on high power for 2 to 3 minutes, until warm. Add to rice and mix thoroughly.

3. Divide pork mixture and cheese between tortillas. Fold tortillas (as on page 39). Serve warm.

Baked Pasta *and* Pasta Frittata

| | 2
servings
pasta | 2
servings
frittata |

You love pasta, but your roommates judge if you eat it every night. Solution: hide it in a frittata.

Baked Pasta

$^1/_2$ pound penne pasta, cooked according to
    package directions
$^1/_4$ cup grated pecorino or other hard cheese
$^1/_2$ teaspoon minced garlic
$^1/_2$ teaspoon salt
5 ounces frozen chopped spinach, cooked
    according to package directions
1 12- to 15-ounce jar marinara sauce
$^3/_4$ cup shredded mozzarella cheese
Cooking spray

1. Preheat oven to 400°F. In a large bowl, combine
   pasta, pecorino, garlic, salt, spinach, sauce, and
   half of the mozzarella.

2. Transfer half of the mixture to a container and let cool. Cover and refrigerate for up to 3 days for use in frittata (below).

3. Spray a 9-inch square pan with cooking spray. Place pasta mixture in pan and sprinkle with remaining mozzarella. Cover loosely with aluminum foil.

4. Bake for 20 minutes. Uncover and bake for 10 more minutes, until cheese bubbles at the edges.

Pasta Frittata

Reserved pasta mixture
4 large eggs
$1/2$ cup shredded mozzarella cheese

1. Preheat oven to 400°F. In a large bowl, whisk eggs. Add pasta mixture and mix to combine.

2. Spray a 9-inch square pan with cooking spray. Place pasta mixture in pan. Sprinkle cheese evenly over the top. Bake uncovered for about 20 minutes, until the top is set and the edges are golden brown.

Lentils and Rice *and* Lentil Soup

	2	2
	servings	bowls
	lentils and rice	soup

Lentils are always a good choice, whether you're looking for something nutritious, something inexpensive, something tasty, or your next creative writing prompt. Just think of the odes that lentils could—some would say should—inspire!

Lentils and Rice

1 cup dried lentils

$1/2$ cup white rice

$1/2$ teaspoon ground cumin

$1/2$ teaspoon salt

$1/4$ teaspoon ground cayenne pepper, or to taste

$1/2$ cup shredded carrots

2 tablespoons olive oil

1 large red onion, thinly sliced

1. In a large saucepan over high heat, bring 3 cups water to a boil. Add lentils and return to a boil. Cover, reduce heat to a simmer, and cook for about 30 minutes, until lentils are soft.

2. Stir in rice, cumin, salt, cayenne, and 1 additional cup water. Cover and cook for about 20 minutes, until rice is tender. Remove from heat. Stir in carrots, cover, and let stand.

3. In a medium skillet, heat oil over medium heat for 1 minute. Add onion. Cook, stirring frequently, for about 10 minutes, until onion is soft and browned.

4. Transfer $1\frac{1}{2}$ cups of the lentil mixture and 2 tablespoons of onions to a container and let cool. Cover and refrigerate for up to three days for use in soup (page 86).

5. Divide remaining lentils and rice between 2 bowls and top with onions. Serve warm.

Lentil Soup

Reserved cooked lentils, rice, and onions
1 14.5- to 15-ounce can diced tomatoes
1 cup chicken broth
$1/2$ teaspoon salt, or to taste
$1/4$ teaspoon ground black pepper, or to taste
$1/2$ cup plain Greek-style yogurt

1. In a large saucepan, combine all ingredients except yogurt. Bring to a boil over medium-high heat, stirring occasionally.

2. Divide soup between 2 bowls and top each with $1/4$ cup yogurt.

Chicken Soup *and* Chicken Pot Pie

2	2
servings	*servings*
soup	*pot pie*

When it's so cold that all you want to do is to curl up with the TV remote, these recipes will give you the energy to brave the bitter walk to class.

Chicken Soup

    1 tablespoon oil

    2 large chicken breasts (or 3 cups cooked chicken)

    1 14.5- to 15-ounce can chicken broth

    1 cup diced carrots

    1 cup diced zucchini

    1 cup diced potatoes

    1 teaspoon salt

    $1/2$ teaspoon ground black pepper

    $1/2$ teaspoon dried thyme

1. In a large skillet, heat oil over medium-high heat for 1 minute.

2. Add chicken, cover, and lower heat to medium. Cook on each side for about 8 minutes, or until chicken is no longer pink in the center and the internal temperature is 160°F. Transfer chicken to a plate, let cool, and chop into bite-sized pieces. Transfer half of the chicken (about $1^1/2$ cups) to a storage container. Cover and refrigerate for up to 3 days for use in Chicken Pot Pie (below).

3. In a large saucepan, combine the rest of the ingredients with $^1/_2$ cup water and bring to a boil over medium-high heat.

4. Add chicken to saucepan and lower heat to a simmer. Cook for at least an hour, or until vegetables are tender. Serve hot.

Chicken Pot Pie

5 ounces frozen peas and carrots
3 tablespoons butter
3 tablespoons flour
3 tablespoons minced onion
$^1/_2$ teaspoon salt
$^1/_4$ teaspoon ground black pepper
1 cup chicken broth

1/3 cup milk
Reserved 1 1/2 cups chopped chicken from soup
Cooking spray
1 16-ounce can biscuit dough

1. Preheat oven to 350°F. Cook carrots and peas according to package instructions and set aside.

2. In a medium saucepan over low heat, melt butter. Using a wooden spoon, stir in flour, onion, salt, and pepper. Cook for about 2 minutes, until mixture is bubbly.

3. Turn off heat. Stir in broth and milk. Turn heat to medium-low and bring to a boil, stirring constantly. Boil for about 1 minute and stir in chicken and vegetables. Turn off heat.

4. Spray a 9-by-5-inch loaf pan with cooking spray. Spread chicken filling in the pan. Unroll biscuit dough and lay over filling to cover. (Wrap extra dough in plastic wrap and refrigerate for up to 2 days to use with another meal.)

5. Bake for 25 to 30 minutes, or until topping is golden brown.

DORMMATE
DINNERS

Pasta with Meatballs

▓▓ | 4
▓▓ | *servings*

Sometimes it's the small things—like homemade meatballs—that really make a difference to a friend who's stressed or homesick. This recipe can easily be doubled to feed more people. Serve it with warm Italian bread and a salad to really wow the crowd.

Sauce:

1 teaspoon minced garlic
2 tablespoons olive oil
3 ounces tomato paste
$1/2$ teaspoon salt or to taste
$1/2$ teaspoon ground black pepper or to taste
$1/2$ teaspoon Italian seasoning or to taste
1 15-ounce can tomato sauce
1 15-ounce can diced tomatoes

1. In medium saucepan cook garlic in oil over medium-high heat for $1^{1}/_{2}$ to 2 minutes, or until garlic is fragrant.

2. Add tomato paste, salt, pepper, and Italian seasoning and cook, stirring constantly, for 2 minutes.

3. Turn heat to low. Add tomato sauce and diced tomatoes. Stir until combined. Simmer for 30 to 60 minutes, until sauce reaches your desired thickness. Stir every 10 minutes to make sure sauce does not stick to bottom of pan.

Meatballs:

   1 pound lean ground beef
   ½ cup seasoned bread crumbs
   1 egg
   2 tablespoons olive oil

1. In a large mixing bowl place beef, bread crumbs, and egg. Mix with your hands until thoroughly combined. (Your hands will get messy.)

2. Divide mixture into 10 equal parts. With your hands, roll each part into a ball. Place balls on a plate. Immediately wash your hands.

3. In a large frying pan, heat oil over medium heat for 2 minutes. Tilt pan around so oil coats the bottom.

Add meatballs, being careful not to crowd them together. Cook in batches if necessary. Cover, leaving the lid slightly ajar so hot air can escape, and cook, turning meatballs with a spatula a few times, until browned on all sides.

4. Remove pan from heat when the meatballs' internal temperature reaches at least 160°F.

Pasta:

4 servings dried spaghetti or your favorite pasta

1. Cook pasta according to package directions. Drain and serve immediately with sauce and meatballs.

Ramen Done Right

4
servings

The quintessential easy college meal is packaged ramen noodles. They're cheap, tasty, and take about 30 seconds to make. These versions are even more flavorful—and nutritious!—courtesy of extra ingredients and a few minutes of prep.

Chicken Ramen

Cooking spray
1 pound chicken breast, cut into strips
3 cups chicken broth
1 cup shredded carrots
3 green onions, sliced
1 teaspoon salt, or to taste
1 teaspoon ground black pepper
$^1/_3$ cup golden raisins
$^1/_4$ cup sliced almonds
8 ounces rice noodles

1. Spray a medium frying pan with cooking spray. Add

chicken to pan and cook over medium heat for 6 minutes. Flip chicken and cook for an additional 6 minutes. Turn off heat and set aside.

2. In a medium saucepan, bring broth, carrots, green onions, salt, pepper, raisins, and almonds to a boil.

3. Meanwhile, cut chicken into bite-sized pieces. Add to broth and lower heat to a simmer.

4. In a large saucepan over high heat, bring 4 quarts of water to a boil. Add noodles and boil, stirring occasionally, for 2 to 4 minutes, until tender. Drain. Add noodles to broth and stir to combine all ingredients. Divide among 4 bowls. Serve warm.

Beef Ramen

Cooking spray
1 pound beef tenderloin, cut into strips
3 cups beef broth
1 green bell pepper, sliced
3 green onions, sliced
1 teaspoon minced garlic
1 teaspoon soy sauce
1 teaspoon ground black pepper

$^{1}/_{2}$ teaspoon minced ginger
8 ounces rice noodles

1. Spray a medium frying pan with cooking spray. Add beef and cook over medium heat for 5 minutes. With tongs, flip meat and cook for an additional 5 minutes. Turn off heat and set aside.

2. In a medium saucepan over medium heat, bring broth, peppers, green onions, garlic, soy sauce, black pepper, and ginger to a boil. Meanwhile, cut beef into bite-sized pieces.

3. Add beef to broth and lower heat to a simmer.

4. In a large saucepan over high heat, bring 4 quarts of water to a boil. Add noodles and boil, stirring occasionally, for 2 to 4 minutes, until tender. Drain. Add noodles to broth and stir to combine all ingredients. Divide among 4 bowls. Serve warm.

Pasta, Sausage, and Peppers

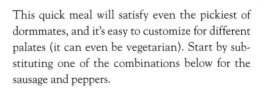

4
servings

This quick meal will satisfy even the pickiest of dormmates, and it's easy to customize for different palates (it can even be vegetarian). Start by substituting one of the combinations below for the sausage and peppers.

> 1 pound dried pasta such as ziti, penne, or rotini
> ¼ cup plus 2 tablespoons olive oil, divided
> 1 pound sausage links
> 1 teaspoon minced garlic
> 2 large bell peppers, sliced
> 1 medium onion, sliced
> ½ cup grated Parmesan cheese
> Salt to taste

1. In a large frying pan over medium heat, warm 1 tablespoon of the oil for 1 minute. Add sausage and cook, turning occasionally with tongs, until browned on all sides. When the internal temperature reaches 160°F, transfer sausage to a plate to let it cool.

2. In the same frying pan, add 1 teaspoon of the oil, peppers, onions, and garlic and cook about 5 to 6 minutes, until softened. Remove from heat and set aside.

3. In a large saucepan bring 4 to 5 quarts water to a boil. Cook pasta according to package directions. Meanwhile, slice sausage into bite-sized rounds. Drain pasta, reserving $1/2$ cup of the pasta water.

4. Return pasta to saucepan and add the remaining oil, cheese, sausage, and vegetables. Mix thoroughly with a large spoon. If the mixture seems dry add a bit of the reserved pasta water. Serve immediately.

Other Tasty Combinations

- Substitute 1 pound chicken for sausage and 2 cups broccoli for peppers.
- Replace sausage with 1 pound ham and swap 2 cups peas for peppers.
- Vegetarian: omit meat and cook $1/2$ cup each peppers, mushrooms, broccoli, and carrots with the garlic and onions.

Chicken, Mashed Potatoes, and Green Beans

4
servings

It may not be exactly like Mom's, but this hearty, warm meal will put a smile on your face. Make it your own by experimenting with the spices while panfrying the chicken—try lemon juice and garlic salt, taco seasoning, or lime juice and honey.

A few tablespoons olive oil

2 pounds chicken breast

2 pounds potatoes, peeled and quartered

4 tablespoons butter

1 teaspoon salt, or to taste

$1/2$ teaspoon ground black pepper

1 cup milk, or to taste

12 ounces steam-in-bag green beans

Salt to taste

Ground black pepper to taste

1. In a large skillet, heat oil over medium-high heat for 1 minute. Add chicken and cover. Cook for 8

minutes per side, or until no longer pink in the center. Turn off heat and cover to keep warm.

2. Fill a large saucepan with 4 to 5 quarts of water and add potatoes. Bring to a boil over high heat and cook until potatoes can be pierced easily with a fork.

3. Drain liquid. Add butter, salt, pepper, and milk and use a hand mixer to whip. Cover and set aside.

4. Microwave beans according to package instructions. Season with salt and pepper. Serve immediately with chicken and mashed potatoes.

Pizza

🔲 | 4
servings

The ultimate party food doesn't have to be ordered. With a little preparation—letting the dough rise while you're at class—you can make it fresh. If you use frozen dough, let it thaw in the fridge overnight.

    2 tablespoons olive oil
    16 ounces pizza dough (if frozen, thawed in the
        refrigerator overnight)
    $1/2$ 15-ounce can pizza sauce
    8 ounces shredded mozzarella cheese
    Toppings of your choice (optional)

1. Before you go to class, place oil in a large mixing bowl. Place dough on top and flip it a couple of times to coat it completely. Cover bowl tightly with plastic wrap and leave on the counter at room temperature for at least 2 hours.

2. Remove plastic and punch down the risen dough. Let it rest for 5 minutes.

3. Preheat oven to 450°F, or as high as it goes. Place dough in the middle of a 14$\frac{1}{2}$-by-$\frac{1}{2}$-inch round pizza pan. Stretch dough a little at a time until it reaches the edge of the pan all around. This will take a few minutes. Stretch firmly, but don't tear holes in the dough.

4. With a spoon, spread sauce over dough. Sprinkle cheese over sauce, covering as much of the surface as possible. Add toppings, if desired (see below).

5. Bake for about 22 minutes, or until cheese is melted and crust is golden brown. Slice into 8 pieces and serve immediately.

Topping Ideas

- 4 ounces sliced pepperoni
- 1 green pepper, thinly sliced, with 5 ounces sliced mushrooms
- 1 cup cubed ham and 1 cup drained canned pineapple chunks
- $\frac{1}{2}$ pound cooked ground meat
- 1 7-ounce jar roasted red peppers, drained, with 1 cup feta cheese

Macaroni and Cheese

4 servings | **6 to 8** servings with mix-ins

The ultimate comfort food. Although the little boxes with the packet of powdered cheese are tempting, making your own isn't hard (and is much more delicious). For variety, stir in some mix-ins from the list below.

4 tablespoons butter
4 tablespoons flour
3 cups milk
8 ounces shredded cheddar cheese
1 teaspoon salt, or to taste
$1/2$ teaspoon black ground pepper, or to taste
1 pound dried pasta such as elbows, campanelle, or cellentani

1. In a large saucepan over medium heat, melt butter. Add flour and stir constantly for 2 minutes. (This is called making a roux.) Slowly add milk and continue stirring until smooth. Cook until mixture boils. Lower heat slightly and add cheese, salt, and pep-

per, stirring until smooth and slightly thickened.

2. Meanwhile in a large saucepan, bring 4 to 5 quarts water to a boil. Cook pasta according to package directions.

3. Drain pasta and add to cheese sauce. Stir to coat pasta with sauce. Serve immediately.

Mix-Ins

Adding one of the following will increase the yield to 6 to 8 servings.

- 2 cups cubed cooked ham and 1 cup cooked peas
- 2 cups cubed cooked chicken and 1 cup bite-sized broccoli florets
- $\frac{1}{2}$ pound taco meat (see page 72)
- $\frac{1}{2}$ pound cooked bacon cut into bite-sized pieces

DATE-NIGHT
DINNERS

Lemon Chicken with Roasted Potatoes

| 2
servings

Although this recipe is a little complicated, each part is relatively simple and the whole can be completed in less than an hour. The flavors are sure to please, and you'll still have time to dress for dinner.

Roasted Potatoes:

3 medium red potatoes, chopped into bite-sized pieces
$1/4$ cup olive oil
$1/2$ teaspoon salt
$1/4$ teaspoon ground black pepper

1. Preheat oven to 425°F. Combine potatoes, oil, salt, and pepper in a 9-inch square pan and stir until potatoes are evenly coated with oil. Don't crowd them. Cover tightly with foil.

2. Bake for 45 minutes, or until potatoes break apart easily when pierced with a fork. Set aside and keep warm. Leave oven on; the chicken cooks at the same temperature as the potatoes.

Roasted Chicken:

1 tablespoon butter
$^2/_3$ cup flour
$^1/_2$ teaspoon salt
$^1/_4$ teaspoon ground black pepper
$^3/_4$ to 1 pound chicken breasts

1. Place butter in a 9-inch square pan and put in a 425°F oven to melt.

2. On a dinner plate mix flour, salt, and pepper with a fork. Toss chicken in flour mixture until fully coated.

3. Using an oven mitt, open the oven and tilt the pan to coat the bottom with butter. Arrange chicken in pan. Bake for 25 minutes. Using a metal spatula, flip chicken and bake for an additional 20 minutes, or until the internal temperature is between 165°F and 175°F.

Lemon Sauce:

1 tablespoon olive oil
2 teaspoons minced garlic
$3/4$ cup chicken broth
$1/4$ cup lemon juice
1 teaspoon crushed red pepper flakes
$1/2$ teaspoon salt

1. In a small saucepan over medium heat, cook oil and garlic uncovered for about 2 minutes, or until garlic is fragrant.

2. Add broth, juice, red pepper, and salt. Bring to a boil and cook for 2 minutes. Remove from heat

3. Pour over chicken and potatoes before serving.

Roasted Vegetables

You can roast a variety of vegetables following the instructions on page 108 for the Roasted Potatoes. Broccoli, carrots, brussels sprouts, root vegetables like parsnips or turnips, zucchini—the sky's the limit. Start checking vegetables for doneness after about 15 minutes by poking them with a fork. When cooked, they will be tender and slightly charred at the edges. Exact times will vary depending on the vegetables, how small you cut them, and how your oven is calibrated.

Steak and Onions

2
servings

A properly cooked steak is the best way to appeal to the meat lover in your life. Unless you have access to a grill, you'll be panfrying this steak, so use a cut that's well suited for this method—New York strip, sirloin, or tenderloin.

2 onions, thinly sliced
2 tablespoons olive oil, divided
1 pound steak, cut into 2 pieces
1 teaspoon salt

1. In a large skillet over medium-high heat, cook the onions in 1 tablespoon of the oil until browned.

2. Season steak with salt. Move onions to one side of the pan. Add the remaining tablespoon of oil to the other side and place steaks in pan. Cook, uncovered, for about 6 to 7 minutes per side, or until the internal temperature is at least 145°F. Remove from heat, cover pan, and let meat rest for 3 minutes before serving.

How to Keep Food Warm

Have you finished cooking dinner and your roommates just called to say they would be 20 minutes late? Don't panic. Here are two methods to save the day.

Method 1: Oven
Heat the oven to 145°F–150°F. Put the food on an oven-safe plate and cover tightly with aluminum foil. Place in the oven.

Method 2: Double Broiler
Fill the bottom pot halfway with water. Put the food in the top pan and cover with the lid. Keep it on the lowest heat setting.

Don't have a double-boiler? No problem. Fill a large saucepan halfway with water. Transfer the meal to a metal bowl larger than the pan, cover with foil and place bowl on top of pan. Set pan over low heat until your guests arrive.

Pasta with Mushrooms and Cheese

 2
servings

This vegetarian dish may come together quickly, but it tastes like you spent hours in the kitchen. Serve with a loaf of Italian bread and your favorite salad. Remember to accept compliments gracefully.

1/4 cup plus 1 tablespoon olive oil, divided
1/4 cup minced onions
1 teaspoon minced garlic
1/2 pound sliced mushrooms
8 ounces medium-sized pasta such as ziti
1/2 cup grated Parmesan cheese
Salt to taste

1. In a medium frying pan over medium heat, warm 1 tablespoon of the oil for 1 minute. Add onions and garlic and cook for 2 to 3 minutes. Lower heat to medium-low and add mushrooms. Cook for an additional 5 to 6 minutes.

2. Meanwhile, in a 5-quart saucepan bring $2^1/_2$ quarts water to a boil. Cook pasta according to package directions. Drain, reserving $^1/_2$ cup of the pasta water.

3. In the saucepan combine pasta, the remaining $^1/_4$ cup oil, cheese, salt, and vegetables. Mix thoroughly with a large spoon. If the mixture seems dry add a bit of the saved pasta water. Serve immediately.

Salmon with Oven-Roasted Asparagus

2
servings

Salmon is classy, tasty, and a great choice for a lighter meal. If you have two 9-inch baking pans, you can finesse the preparation. Put the salmon in the oven first, and after 10 minutes add the asparagus. They'll be done at the same time, and you'll look like a pro.

Salmon

2 tablespoons olive oil, divided
12 ounces salmon fillets
1 teaspoon salt, or to taste
$^1/_2$ teaspoon ground black pepper

1. Preheat oven to 350°F. Pour 1 tablespoon of the oil in a 9-inch square pan. Arrange salmon in pan, drizzle with the remaining oil, and sprinkle with salt and pepper.

2. Bake for 20 minutes. Salmon is done when completely opaque and when the thickest part of the fillet flakes easily with a fork. The internal temperature should reach 145°F.

Asparagus

   1/2 pound asparagus
   2 to 3 tablespoons olive oil, divided
   1/2 teaspoon salt
   1/4 teaspoon ground black pepper
   1 teaspoon minced garlic

1. Snap off and discard the tough bottom section of each asparagus stalk.

2. Pour 1 tablespoon of the oil in a 9-inch square pan. Arrange asparagus in pan in a single layer, drizzle with the remaining oil, and sprinkle with salt, pepper, and garlic.

3. Bake for 10 minutes, or until tender, and serve.

Shrimp Scampi with Linguini

  | 2
servings

Serve this flavor-packed entrée with some good bread to soak up the sauce.

   8 ounces frozen cooked shrimp, peeled
   8-ounce box linguini
   2 tablespoons olive oil
   3 teaspoons minced garlic
   2 teaspoons Italian seasoning
   1 tablespoon cornstarch
   1 cup chicken broth
   Pinch of salt, or to taste
   Pinch of ground black pepper, or to taste

1. Fill a large bowl with cold water and add shrimp. While they are defrosting, boil 2$\frac{1}{2}$ quarts water in a 5-quart saucepan and cook pasta according to package directions. Drain, return to pan, cover, and set aside.

2. In a large skillet over medium heat, warm oil, garlic, and Italian seasoning for 2 to 3 minutes.

Meanwhile, in a small bowl, dissolve cornstarch in chicken broth. Stir until smooth.

3. Add broth mixture to pan and simmer for 3 to 4 minutes, until sauce thickens slightly.

4. Add defrosted shrimp pan and cook for 3 to 4 minutes, until they are opaque and bright pink. Add salt and pepper.

5. Divide pasta between two plates. Top each with shrimp scampi and serve immediately.

No-Cook Appetizer Platter

2
servings

Serve this selection of starters to a larger crowd before a full meal. It can also double as a romantic dinner for two. Everything can be bought in most supermarkets, but feel free to make substitutions according to what's available and what you and your guest(s) enjoy. Part of the fun of eating with someone is sharing your tastes and exploring new flavors together.

6 loaves pita
$1/2$ pound feta cheese
$1/2$ pound gouda cheese
$1/2$ pound mozzarella
1 8.8-ounce box whole grain crackers
1 10-ounce jar kalamata olives
1 10-ounce jar green olives
1 12-ounce jar roasted peppers
2 or 3 10-ounce containers hummus
   in a variety of flavors

1. Cut pitas into quarters. Cut cheeses into cubes.

2. Place ingredients in small bowls or plates and arrange them on a tablecloth-covered table. If desired, light a couple of candles, and voilà! Instant romance.

Picnic Time: Skip the serveware and leave everything in its container. Pack appetizers into a basket with a blanket, plates, and flatware, and have a picnic at a park or beach.

"There is no love sincerer than the love of food."

—*George Bernard Shaw*

Turkey Bacon Salad with Ranch Dressing

1
serving

This salad will get you through the day. Turkey, bacon, cheese: protein, protein, protein!

> 1/4 head lettuce
> 1 cup chopped cooked turkey
> 2 slices crisp bacon (page 40), crumbled
> 1/2 cup shredded Monterey Jack cheese
> Ranch Dressing to taste

1. Wash and dry lettuce (see page 66). With clean hands or a knife, tear or cut into bite-sized pieces. Place in a bowl.

2. Top with turkey, bacon, and cheese.

3. Toss with dressing and serve.

Ranch Dressing

About
1/2
cup

This classic dressing is sure to please even your pickiest friends. And don't worry about the unusual ingredient; you can always freeze leftover buttermilk.

1/4 cup buttermilk
2 tablespoons nonfat plain Greek yogurt
1/2 tablespoon fresh or 1/2 teaspoon dried chives
1/2 teaspoon cider vinegar
1/4 teaspoon salt
1/4 teaspoon sugar

1. In a small bowl, whisk together ingredients with a wire whisk until smooth. Serve. Refrigerate any leftovers, covered, for up to 3 days.

SWEETS AND
SNACKS

Icebox Cake

| **8**
servings

This cake requires no baking and can be made in a short time. Once you've assembled the layers of creamy chocolate pudding sandwiched between crunchy graham crackers, set it in the refrigerator before you go to class. In a few hours it will be ready to share with friends as a cool treat on a warm day.

1 1.4-ounce box chocolate pudding mix
2 cups milk
1 14.4-ounce box chocolate graham crackers
1 8-ounce tub whipped topping

1. Make pudding with the milk according to package directions. Refrigerate until set, about 5 minutes.

2. Place two layers of graham crackers on the bottom of a 9-inch square baking pan, using a knife to cut the crackers to fit, if necessary.

3. Spread half the pudding on top of graham crackers. Spread one-third of the whipped topping on top of pudding. Top with another layer of graham crackers.

4. Repeat step 3. Top the final layer of graham crackers with the remaining whipped topping.

5. Cover pan loosely with plastic wrap and refrigerate for at least 4 hours. Use a metal spatula to cut and serve ice box cake.

No-Bake Mini Cheesecakes

	6
	mini cheesecakes

No-bake and *cheesecake* are two of our favorite words. Put them together and you have this tasty treat that is delicious on its own as well as the perfect companion to your favorite toppings.

    4 ounces cream cheese, softened
    4 ounces whipped topping, room temperature
    $\frac{1}{2}$ cup sour cream
    $\frac{3}{4}$ cup granulated sugar
    1 teaspoon vanilla extract
    6 vanilla wafers or other round cookie that fits in
        the bottom of cupcake liners
    6 strawberries, cleaned and hulled, and/or topping
        of your choice

1. In a medium bowl, mix cream cheese, whipped topping, sour cream, sugar, and vanilla until well combined.

2. Place 6 foil cupcake liners in a cupcake pan. Put a cookie in the bottom of each, cutting them to fit if necessary.

3. Divide the batter evenly among cupcake liners. Refrigerate for at least 4 hours.

4. Top each cheesecake with a strawberry.

Optional Toppings

- Blueberries, raspberries, or pieces of other fresh fruit

- Chocolate syrup, strawberry syrup, or honey

- Any flavor fruit preserves

- Candy-coated chocolates or your favorite candy bar, crushed up

"Because you don't live near a bakery doesn't mean you have to go without cheesecake."

—Hedy Lamarr

Chocolate Chip Cookie Bars

🍳 | **16** bars

Everyone loves chocolate chip cookies. This recipe cuts down on the time spent spooning and rolling dough into individual portions. All the dough is baked in a pan and then cut into bars.

Baking spray
1 1/2 cups all-purpose flour
1/2 teaspoon baking powder
1/2 teaspoon salt
1/2 cup (1 stick) salted butter or margarine, softened
1/2 cup granulated sugar
1/2 cup packed light brown sugar
1 egg
1 teaspoon vanilla extract
1 cup chocolate chips

1. Preheat oven to 350°F and position a rack in the center of the oven. Spray a 9-inch square baking pan with baking spray.

2. In a small bowl, combine flour, baking powder, and salt. Set aside.

3. In a medium bowl combine butter and sugars with a large spoon or hand mixer until thoroughly combined. Add egg and vanilla. Mix, occasionally scraping down the sides of the bowl, for about 2 minutes.

4. Add half the flour mixture to butter mixture and mix until combined. Repeat with the remaining flour mixture. Stir in chocolate chips.

5. Pour dough into prepared pan and place in center of the oven. Bake for 20 to 25 minutes, until the top is dry and golden brown and the sides pull away from the pan.

6. Place pan on stove top to cool for 10 minutes. Invert it onto a plate and cut into bars.

Brownies

🔲 | **16**
brownies

If you're in the mood for chocolate, this recipe will hit the spot. You can wrap up a single brownie to enjoy with lunch or put a scoop of ice cream and some chocolate syrup on top for a decadent dessert. Change things up by stirring one of the mix-ins into the batter.

Baking spray
$1/2$ cup all-purpose flour
$1/2$ cup baking cocoa
$1/2$ teaspoon baking powder
$1/4$ teaspoon salt
$1/4$ cup ($1/2$ stick) salted butter or margarine, melted
$3/4$ cup granulated sugar
2 eggs
$1/4$ cup vegetable oil
1 teaspoon vanilla extract
Optional mix-ins: 1 cup mini marshmallows; $1/2$ cup creamy peanut butter; $1/2$ cup chocolate chips or chopped nuts

1. Preheat oven to 350°F and position a rack in the center of the oven. Spray a 9-inch square baking pan with baking spray.

2. In small bowl, combine flour, cocoa, baking powder, and salt. Set aside.

3. In a medium bowl, beat butter, sugar, eggs, oil, and vanilla with a large spoon or a hand mixer until thoroughly mixed.

4. Add half the flour mixture to butter mixture and mix until combined. Repeat with the rest of the flour mixture, scraping down sides of bowl with a rubber spatula.

5. Pour mixture into prepared pan and bake in the center of the oven for 20 to 25 minutes, until the sides of the brownies pull away from the pan and the top is dry.

6. Place pan on the stove top to cool for 10 minutes. Invert it onto a plate and cut brownies into squares.

Cake in a Cup

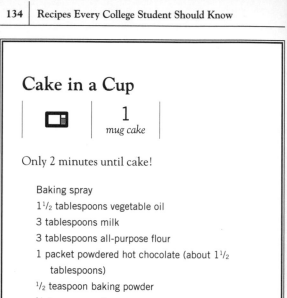

1
mug cake

Only 2 minutes until cake!

Baking spray
1¹/₂ tablespoons vegetable oil
3 tablespoons milk
3 tablespoons all-purpose flour
1 packet powdered hot chocolate (about 1¹/₂
   tablespoons)
¹/₂ teaspoon baking powder
¹/₈ teaspoon salt
2 tablespoons chocolate chips

1. Spray a microwave-safe mug with baking spray.
   Add remaining ingredients except chocolate chips.
   Mix until smooth. Add chocolate chips and stir until
   evenly distributed.

2. Microwave on high power for 1:10. It will rise but
   should not spill over. When done, the cake should
   look dry on top. If not, microwave for 10-second
   intervals until it does.

No-Bake Chewy Granola Bars

16
granola bars

Rolled oats make this snack healthy. Chocolate chips make it yummy.

Baking spray
$^1/_2$ cup creamy peanut butter
$^1/_2$ cup honey
2 cups old-fashioned rolled oats
1 cup sliced almonds
1 cup chocolate chips

1. Line a 9-inch square pan with plastic wrap and spray plastic with baking spray.

2. In a microwave-safe bowl combine peanut butter and honey and microwave for 10 seconds on high power. Stir to combine thoroughly. Add oats, almonds, and chocolate chips and stir until everything is mixed and coated.

3. Pour mixture into prepared pan and refrigerate for 15 minutes, until set. Cut into bars.

Microwave Potato Chips

About
2
cups

You'll be surprised how good fresh potato chips taste!

1 medium red potato, peeled and cut in half
Cooking spray
1 teaspoon salt or to taste

1. Use a vegetable peeler to slice potato in uniformly thin slices.

2. Line a microwave-safe plate with wax paper. Spray wax paper with cooking spray.

3. Lay potato slices on wax paper. Sprinkle with salt.

4. Microwave on high power for 3 minutes. The slices should be golden brown and dry to the touch. If they aren't, microwave for additional 10-second increments until they are done. You may want to eat them right off the plate, but give them a minute to cool.

Popcorn

About
5
cups popped

Packaged microwavable popcorn is convenient, but this recipe is healthier, cheaper, and made in the same amount of time—with hardly more effort.

  1/4 cup unpopped popcorn kernels
  1 brown paper lunch bag
  Cooking spray
  Salt to taste

1. Put popcorn kernels in bag. Fold over the top flap 3 or 4 times.

2. Microwave on high for $1\frac{1}{2}$ to $2\frac{1}{2}$ minutes. Stop the microwave as soon as the popping slows down.

3. Transfer popcorn to a serving bowl. Spray with cooking spray and sprinkle with salt. Use a spoon to gently stir a few times. Repeat spraying and salting to taste.

Chocolate-Covered Popcorn

About

4

cups

You've been writing a paper for hours, and now you're craving something salty, sweet, and crunchy. Fortunately, chocolate-covered popcorn is here to save your study break! Be careful not to overcook the chocolate. Burnt chocolate smells worse than burnt popcorn, and you don't need the RA knocking on your door at 1 a.m.

1 1.75-ounce package microwavable popcorn, or 1
    recipe Popcorn (page 137)
1 1/2 cups chocolate chips or white chocolate chips

1. Make popcorn according to package directions or the recipe on page 137. Don't walk away from the microwave. As soon as the popping slows down, stop the microwave. Take out bag and let it cool.

2. Put chocolate chips in a microwave-safe bowl. Microwave on high power for 1 minute. Stir. If chocolate is not smooth and creamy, continue to micro-

wave for 30-second intervals, stirring after each,
until fully melted.

3. Transfer popcorn to a 13-by-9-inch baking sheet
   or a plate that will fit in your refrigerator. Pick out
   and discard unpopped kernels. Pat popcorn into a
   single layer.

4. Drizzle melted chocolate onto popcorn, covering
   popcorn as much as possible.

5. Place pan in refrigerator for about 10 minutes.
   Remove from fridge and break chocolate-covered
   popcorn into bite-sized pieces.

Optional Mix-Ins

Toss one of the following with popcorn in step 3
after discarding the unpopped kernels.

- 1 cup mini marshmallows
- 1 cup candy-coated chocolates
- 2 cups broken pretzels
- 1 cup your favorite sweet cereal

Nachos

6
servings

At their simplest, nachos are tortilla chips topped with melted cheese and sliced jalapeños. But you can include enough toppings to turn this snack into an entrée. They're an easy option to serve when you have friends over. With so many great flavors, they have something for everyone.

   1 13-ounce bag tortilla chips
   1 15-ounce can chili, with or without beans
   1 16-ounce jar cheese sauce
   4 ounces sliced olives
   4 ounces sliced jalapeño chiles
   1 16-ounce jar salsa
   8 ounces guacamole
   8 ounces sour cream

1. On a large serving platter spread chips in a single layer.

2. In a microwave-safe bowl, microwave chili on high power for 2 to 3 minutes.

3. In another microwave-safe bowl, microwave cheese sauce on high power for 2 to 3 minutes.

4. Spoon chili and cheese sauce over tortilla chips. Sprinkle olives and jalapeños on top of cheese sauce. Top with salsa, guacamole, and sour cream. Serve immediately.

Metric Conversion Charts

Volume

U.S.	Metric
¼ tsp	1.25 ml
½ tsp	2.5 ml
1 tsp	5 ml
1 tbsp (3 tsp)	15 ml
1 fl oz (2 tbsp)	30 ml
¼ cup	60 ml
⅓ cup	80 ml
½ cup	120 ml
1 cup	240 ml
1 pint (2 cups)	480 ml
1 quart (2 pints)	960 ml
1 gallon (4 quarts)	3.84 liters

Weight

U.S.	Metric
1 oz	28 g
4 oz (¼ lb)	113 g
8 oz (½ lb)	227 g
12 oz (¾ lb)	340 g
16 oz (1 lb)	454 g
2.2 lb	1 kg

Length

Inches	Centimeters
¼	0.65
½	1.25
1	2.50
2	5.00
3	7.50
4	10.0
5	12.5

Oven Temperature

Degrees Fahrenheit	Degrees Centigrade	British Gas Marks
200	93	—
250	120	½
275	140	1
300	150	2
325	165	3
350	175	4
375	190	5
400	200	6
450	230	8

Acknowledgments

Thank you to:

Tiffany, the best editor for a first time author like myself, without whom this book would not exist.

Rick, my husband, who ate everything I made as I learned to cook and never complained.

All of the Roses in my life, who each in her own way, showed me how important it is for family and friends to gather around the table, share homemade meals and tell silly stories.